DECIDING TO Soar!
180 Lessons to Catapult Your Life

DECIDING TO Soar!
180 Lessons to Catapult Your Life

SharRon Jamison

DECIDING TO SOAR!

Published by Purposely Created Publishing Group™

Copyright © 2017 SharRon Jamison

All rights reserved.

No part of this book may be reproduced, distributed or transmitted in any form by any means, graphics, electronics, or mechanical, including photocopy, recording, taping, or by any information storage or retrieval system, without permission in writing from the publisher, except in the case of reprints in the context of reviews, quotes, or references.

Printed in the United States of America

ISBN: 978-1-945558-32-0

Special discounts are available on bulk quantity purchases by book clubs, associations and special interest groups. For details email: sales@publishyourgift.com or call (888) 949-6228.

For information logon to: www.PublishYourGift.com

Dedication

To God, my Creator and Cultivator: I love you. I need you and thank you.

To my parents, Reverend Franklin Jamison-Dixon and Dorethia Jamison-Dixon: Thank you for your guidance and encouragement. I love you.

To my only child, Tariq Jamison Abdul-Haqq. Thank you for being my biggest gift and my best supporter. I love you, son!

To my best friend and most faithful supporter, Minister Carrolle Moss (Momma C). You continue to believe in me when I can't believe in myself. I love you.

To my friend and sister, Kim J. King. Thank you for your encouraging words. I appreciate you.

To my friend and sister, V. Chanell Jones. Thank you for reading, editing, praying, and encouraging me during this process. I appreciate you.

To my friend and brother, William G. Bean. Thank you for your support and constant encouragement. You model excellence in all you do. It is a pleasure to serve with you.

Reche T. Abdul-Haqq, Marcella Austin, Carsini Brooks, Yvette D. Bennett, Achleigh-Ambur Lowe: The people who love me despite myself and are always there to help, hope, and heal me. Thank you.

To my pastor, Dr. Kenneth L. Samuel: Thank you for preaching, teaching, and reaching me with your prophetic words. I have learned much from you, Doc. Thank you.

To people who continue to let me into their lives through books, classes, seminars, presentations, interviews, and dinners: I celebrate you. Thank you!

To people who share their platforms, grant me access, connect me to others: Thank you!

Table of Contents

Foreword xi

Personal Growth 1

Faith 43

Success 71

Friendships 109

Relationships 143

About the Author 169

Foreword

So often in life, we need wisdom—poignant insight—that pierces through the busyness, the pervasive noise, and the constant distractions that divert our attention. We need wisdom that provides connection, comfort, counsel, or just plain common sense. We need words of encouragement that erase our worry and strengthen our will so that we can do the work of life, love, loss, and living. We need sage advice that is easy to hear, easy to digest, and easy to apply quickly to our fast-paced, complex lives.

I hope this book provides those messages, succinct lessons, that offer the guidance you need and the reflection you crave. I hope the nuggets shared are short enough to capture your attention, but deep enough that they are relatable and relevant to your respective situations. I hope that these quotes speak to your heart in a way that resonates, illuminates, and elevates your soul.

It is time to change and challenge some of the narratives in our lives that have us living below our own expectations, desires, and needs. It is time to live differently and love fully. It is time to identify what matters most to us so that we can live powerfully, authentically, fearlessly, and peacefully. It is time to Soar! Dare to Soar Higher!

Blessings to you always,

SharRon

Personal Growth

Before you start running, determine if you are running away from something or running toward something.

Where are you going, and why?

Aim before you shoot.

Action without reflection breeds destruction,
disaster, delay, divorce, and damage.
Focus first, aim, and then shoot.

Knowing why helps you
find your way.

Before you start making choices in your life,
know what to choose and why.
You can figure out the
how, when, and where later.

Negative comments and people only enter your space with YOUR permission.

If it doesn't serve or support you, don't grant it access. Remember to guard your heart.

Desperation is never a good look.

Don't wear it. It is a look that doesn't flatter

or honor you.

You are not desperate.

You just have not figured out your way, yet.

When your soul is speaking, listen.
Don't ignore, rationalize, or dismiss your "soul" messages.

Just because it can't be logically explained does not mean that the message is invalid. Sometimes speaking to our souls is the only way that God can speak to us.

People don't really know you.

Don't let the ideas, beliefs, opinions, or perceptions that others have about you hold your mind and body hostage. They don't really know you. And please, don't be contained, confined, entangled, or trapped by the need to be liked by people who don't even like themselves.

Never forget that some people don't possess the capacity to embrace or understand your greatness, and they will always attempt to reduce who you are down to their own level of understanding.

All you can do is live. Just live, and live well.

Your true self will always exceed a person's idea, image, and illusion of who you are.

Only you know you. Others don't have the capacity to fully comprehend what's in your heart, mind, and soul.

Your private pain will show up in public ways.

You are fooling no one. People "see" you because your behavior speaks loudly. Heal your hurts so that you can show up strong.

*If you know it all,
you don't know much.*

Don't let your education keep
you from learning;
there is always more to
learn and know.

Exits and entries, withdrawals and deposits, denials and approvals, additions and subtractions... what do they have in common?

Some blessings are hard to see and understand at first, but trust me, they are blessings nonetheless. Be patient. The reason will be revealed at the appointed time.

Every closure is an opening for something new.

Wise people are grateful for closed

doors even when the reason

for the closure

is not initially revealed.

Being blind is one thing;

refusing to see is another.

Denial and Avoidance: Both give short-term gain but ensure long-term pain. See, acknowledge, and address. It is time to heal.

There is a difference between a transformation and a transfer.

One is a make-over, and one is just a move-over.

Are you making real changes in your life, or are you just applying make-up on top of the mess?

You can't change people; people are who they are.

Change yourself.
Doing and being your best
is already a full-time job.

If you are going to walk on the court, try to score sometimes.

Don't be satisfied to just be in the game. Contribute. Add value. Make a difference and let people know you are there.

Don't aim for average.

Nobody strives to be ordinary; they settle. Why settle when you can be extraordinary? Excellence costs, but pay the price. You are too talented to succumb to mediocrity. Put in the work!

Keeping score is for games, not grown-ups.

What are you gaining by keeping score? Score your OWN success, improvement, and abilities. Your only competition is yourself.

Stop measuring yourself by somebody else's ruler.

Comparing yourself to others is not an accurate reflection of your greatness. Set your own standards and goals based on your own giftedness, and then measure your own progress by your own goals.

It is only true about **YOU** *if you believe it.*

I know what others say about you, BUT what do you believe? Your opinion about you is the only opinion that counts.

You are a little bit of this,

and a little bit of that.

Face it. You are more than one thing, and you feel more than one way at a time. Polarity may be popular, but it is not honest. Sometimes, a situation or experience won't let you choose just one side. Embrace it all.

If ideas are not followed or combined with implementation, nothing happens.

Good ideas and good intentions yield *nothing* with inactivity. Action activates your dreams and accelerates your growth.

People can't see your good heart; they only see your behavior.

The world does not need any more good intentions; it needs actions that will change the trajectory of the world and the ethos of its people.

People will lose interest in your ideas if the only thing you do is talk about them. Do something with them.

Talk is cheap.

Don't wear so many masks that you forget who you truly are.

Do you really know you?

Upward beliefs coupled with downward behaviors will kill your progress and stop your growth every time.

Are you moving up? Elevation requires positive words, work, and will. Don't let your negative habits make you slide down into mediocrity, misery, and mess.

Obedience may be rewarded, but it does not revolutionize.

Great advances in history were made because somebody said "no": no to inequality, no to discrimination, and no to anything that denied dignity to others. For you to follow your political, social, spiritual, and mental truth, you must sometimes say, "No." Be disobedient to social norms, or any practice, philosophy, principle, or plan that fails to honor you. Be disobedient and transform the world.

**See. Be. See.
Be. See. Be:**

The recipe for growth and expansion.

The more you see, the more you know, the more you grow. Exposure expands your mind and reveals what's possible.

You can't handle a high-level situation with a low-level mindset.

Important issues can't be corrected with jealously, greed, ignorance, arrogance, feelings, or the insatiable need for credit. They require communication, creativity, collaboration, and community.

You can't be diplomatic with a dictator.

Push back.

Stand up for yourself.

Don't succumb or be steamrolled by someone else's agenda, policy, temptation, addiction, emotional wound, or belief.

If someone's motives fail to respect you and your truth, push back and keep pushing back until your voice is heard. You must be tough with tyrannical people, places, principalities, practices, and pathologies.

Your inability to work with people

will stunt your own growth.

Building empires requires emotional intelligence.
People don't want to pray or play with people who
are pests, parasites, pirates, or pains.
They want to work with professionals.

> Stand up for yourself,
> or you will be forced
> to sit down
> and stay down.

Are you sitting down in any area of your life? Are you being forced down politically, spiritually, emotionally, or economically? You can't complain about being down if you refuse to stand up. Self-empowerment is a choice.

Your mind is not big enough to mind my business and yours too.

Stay in your lane,
in your house,
in your relationship,
in your life,
and out of my way.

Ease is the enemy of extraordinary.

Ease is a thief that robs you of your true potential. It is an opponent that does not respect your gifts, talents or your divine calling. It's an intruder that undermines your determination, strength, and courage. Watch out for it. It slithers silently into your conscious, slowly shutting down your initiative and disrupting your momentum.

When there is a shortage of courage, there will always be a shortage of integrity.

Cowards never tell the whole truth, and they never do what must be done to honor themselves or others. Are you a coward?

Be brave but think too.

Courage with reflection makes us responsible. Courage without reflection makes us reckless.

Vision
takes us to places that our eyes can't see.

Some things can only be seen through the soul.

So, close your eyes,

quiet your mind,

and see what

God has in store for you.

Liars just lie.

People who will lie to themselves

will always lie to you too.

Don't expect the truth.

When you face opposition, you can either fight, flee, or faint.

What are you going to do?
Your decision will determine your destiny.

Even though you may get by, does not mean that you will get away.

You can manipulate, lie, and steal your way to the top, but eventually the truth about who you are and what you can actually do will be revealed.

Sometimes death is

the only way

that you can live.

You must kill some things—
things like fear, doubt, hate, jealously,
bitterness, and unforgiveness—
so that they will not kill you.

What you internalize you can materialize.

Whatever is inside of your head and your heart can be manifested by your hand.

If you follow someone too closely, you will lose your own way.

Even though a person is an expert, always leave space to develop your own opinion and have your own thoughts.

Some people can't hold water with a cup.

Some people can't keep secrets,
so STOP telling them your business.

Make your own decisions because you are the only person responsible for the outcome.

Don't let people who don't have to live with the consequences make your choices for you. Choose for yourself.

Beliefs Bolster!

Convictions cut through contradictions, contempt, calamity, confusion, convenience, and the need for comfort. A "made-up" mind will find a way to make it.

Don't let former wins prevent future wins.

Success can seduce you into mediocrity, complacency, and arrogance. Don't let success dull your edge. Keep striving.

> Be strong enough to hold on AND be strong enough to let go.

You and you alone are responsible for your worth, wealth, wellness and wholeness.

If you are going to sit at the table, don't be afraid to eat.

You deserve to be there.

You belong.

Eat!

A closed mouth never gets fed.

Faith

God IS...

Whatever you need God to be,

God can be.

Life is mostly an inside job.

Stop searching outside for inside answers.

Everything starts withIN:

INtuition,

INitiative,

INsight,

and INtrospection.

*Are you living in what "IS,"
what "WAS,"
or what
"WILL BE"?*

Where are you living? If you live in yesterday,
you will miss what's happening today and will not
be ready for what's coming tomorrow.
Don't miss valuable moments in your life.

Embrace the truth of who you are and release the lies that society has taught you so that you can be free to create the life you desire.

The press is never free and seldom true; it is manufactured. The person who controls the pen controls what is written, seen, and shared. And what they write is never the truth about who you are, or what you are destined to be. Take the pen and write your own press.

You need Eyesight, Insight, Foresight, and Hindsight to see your way through life.

There are many ways to see. Open your eyes, your mind, your spirit, and your heart to see clearly. Your physical sight can only provide a glimpse—one perspective—of what is present.

We are in a spiritual battle. Expect to fight.

We have political, systematic, economic, demonic, internal, and personal wars to fight. Expect to get hit. Expect to get ambushed. Expect to be shaken. Expect to be surprised. But expect to win!

Words, Wisdom, Work, and Witness.

Listen.

Learn.

Do.

Share.

The true path to success.

Follow your heart, not the herd. Follow your truth, not the tribe. Follow your mind, not the masses. Follow your conscious, not the crowd. Follow your gut, not the group. Follow your purpose, not people. Follow faith, not the flock. Follow God, not gossip.

When someone comes to you and offers unsolicited advice or opinions not based on empirical data, or verifiable information, or without giving the source, give them this response: "I don't run my life by committee; I run it by my own conscious. It matters not what nameless 'they,' 'them,' 'people,' 'she,' 'he,' or other spineless people say, I never feel obligated to go along to get along. I am trying to follow Christ, not the crowd."

Churches should be hospitals for healing souls, not homes for spiritual hits to the heart.

Stop telling people that they are going to hell when you are already creating a hell for them on earth. Don't be only concerned about the afterlife. Ask yourself if you are doing anything to help people live peacefully and fully on earth today.

Stop the gossip you hear with the Gospel you know.

If you don't want people to gossip about you, don't listen when people bring gossip about others to you. Take a stand, because what goes around surely comes around. Let's do better. We owe it to ourselves and to each other.

The church or any faith tradition is not just about getting spiritually high; it is about getting emotionally healed and emotionally whole.

The church is about giving you power to address emotional wounds, toxic people, crazy politics, societal pathology, profits made unfairly, systemic poisons, mass incarceration, unjust legal policies, and any other pharaohs in your life and the world that rob people of dignity, decency, and fail to honor a person's divinity. It is about giving you the power to check, challenge, and change anything that fails to honor God's word and God's way. It is not just about feeling good; it is about doing good.

God gave YOU the vision. Everybody else does not get a voice or a vote.

It is wise to seek counsel, but you never need to gain approval from others when answering your divine call. Validation comes from God.

Advice and approval are not the same thing.

When God gives us visions, dreams, or ideas, many times we seek out others to confirm what God has given us. However, confirmation nor consensus is needed. Move forward. Get advice, yes, but remember that you don't need someone's approval to answer your divine call. God gave you the vision, and when God gives vision, God also gives provision.

> What you constantly yield to, you will eventually yearn for.

Yielding to comfort zones, minimizing traditions, limiting behaviors, toxic relationships, and other belittling beliefs that fail to honor your entire essence will force you to sacrifice your value, vision, and voice. Is that what you desire?

Only beliefs and behaviors that cultivate, cheer, calm, challenge, check, charge, celebrate, and "call" you into greatness deserve you.

Clean it up or heal it up, but please don't dress it up.

I don't care how you try to camouflage your issues or hide your pain; both always show up in your beliefs and behavior. We see you and you see us!

Why not choose a different approach? Instead of dressing up your mistakes, problems, issues, addictions, and pain with money, weaves, lies, clothes, positions, education, titles, religion, and people-pleasing, be honest. Admit the problem and then release what has you bound.

Liberate yourself from IT (whatever it is) so that you can fully LIVE.

Freedom comes with a price. If addiction has you, fear has you, or doubt has you, you are not free to live. You are bound.

The facts never have the last word—faith does.

God changes the facts once you get in motion. Being still will make you miss your blessings and opportunities.

Just because you are alive does not mean that you're living.

Having a pulse without having a purpose is not living. Living happens when you identify your purpose, and decide to fulfill it. Let's live!

God uses willing people, not perfect people.

Don't wait until you have it all together because you will never be perfect. God is not looking for flawless people, only faithful people.

Be prepared! When God gives you a vision, expect villains to surface to frustrate, oppose, discredit, and undermine you.

When you have a divine assignment, expect demonic attacks and demonic assassins from those closest to you.

It means nothing to be spiritually deep if you don't have self-discipline.

It does not matter if you know what's right if you have no interest in doing right! It does not matter if you know thousands of scriptures if you are not willing to live one scripture. Don't judge others and be careful not to drown in your own sense of self-righteousness!

Some people have divine callings but demonic cravings.

Don't let your cravings contradict, cancel out, or cripple your calling. Pray for power and seek help immediately. The world needs your unique gift.

Don't let your "good" overshadow God's "best."

What God has in store for you is better than anything that you can ever have in store for yourself. Don't settle for less when God has promised you the best.

Be the Word,

don't just read the Word.

You may be the only Bible people read.

Represent God well.

> God does not change;
> our understanding of God
> changes.

Our faith evolves as we experience God in new ways, and as we gain new spiritual insight. God is the same yesterday, today, and forever more.

Even Jesus had a "Judas."

Jesus was perfect, and he was betrayed.

So, expect detractors in your camp too.

Borrowed beliefs don't have sustaining power.

You can borrow many things; but some things you need to know for yourself, like God and God's redeeming power.

Don't use God and spirituality as excuses to be lazy.

The Bible is clear: faith without works is dead.

Success

Your first hit may not be the home run, but stay on first base and get ready to run again. The game is not over.

Sometimes, just being in the game sets you up for your next success. Are you in the game? Are you ready to swing the bat?

Progress is Incremental, not Instantaneous.

You may not get all the way to the front on your first try, but get as close as you can. Then, keep moving forward, inch by inch, until you arrive.

You can't achieve big dreams with little motivation, little determination, and little follow-through.

You want success and abundance? Go BIG! Give 100 percent and then when you become depleted, ask God to restore, rejuvenate, and revive you so that you can continue to pursue your dreams.

Refusing to acknowledge a situation does not mean that the situation does not exist.

It's REAL. Acknowledge, Assess, Address, and Move on.

You have to walk through the talk.

So often, we allow our haters to halt our plans and hinder our dreams. Don't listen. Don't let their weak words worry or wound you. Keep walking through the talk as you pursue your dreams and achieve your goals.

You can't have positive thoughts with a negative mind.

What are you thinking about? Life or death? Prosperity or poverty? Growth or stagnation? Truth or lies? Success or failure? Justice or injustice? Love or hate? The quality of your life is a direct reflection of the quality of your thoughts. Change your perspective, and you will change you.

If you don't like the music, then change the song.

We have the power to correct, create, change,
and cultivate what we need and want in our lives.
So why are you dancing to music
(a life, relationship, or job) that no longer
serves or supports you?
CHANGE the song!

Make sure the tongue in your mouth and the tongue in your shoe are moving in the same direction.

Do you do what you say, and say what you do? Are you in alignment? Your words and actions must match to activate your true potential.

Always try before you cry!

Don't be intimidated by the issue.
Don't be overwhelmed by the opportunity.
Don't be consumed with the cause. Try!
Make sure you do your best before you give up,
give out, or give in. You have what it takes to
make your dreams come true.

You can't walk a new path with dirty feet.

Don't let the residue of the past ruin your future. Wash your feet. Remove any dirt, pain, or ill feelings that may sabotage your new beginning.

You can't put big things into small places.

Some people, positions, conversations, beliefs, faith traditions, and behaviors are simply TOO small for you. Don't force yourself into places that fail to honor ALL of who you are and ALL of what you believe.

Don't allow issues to intimidate you or illnesses to psychologically immobilize you.

Trials will come, but so will progress. Don't stop moving, praying, and believing. God is in control.

You can never outrun the truth or your pain, so courageously deal with both.

Running away does not mean that you are free. Stay! Face the "un-face-able" so that you can work to get and stay emotionally free.

What's the difference between a winner and a whiner?

The size of the heart.

How big is your heart? The size of your heart determines your discipline, focus, follow-through, and will power.

Don't make your own prison and then complain about not being free.

We are the ones who limit our lives. If you feel confined or trapped, only you have the key to let yourself out. The key is CHOICE.

Failure is only data, not death!

Failure is not about condemnation; it is about correction. It is not about resignation; it is about evaluation. Fail fast, extract the lesson, and adjust quickly. Use the data to drive future success.

Claim your baggage (issues) and unpack it, so you won't take it with you on other trips.

Why are you still carrying pain, anger, and unforgiveness from your past? Claim it, address it, and then release it. The weight is too heavy to carry for the rest of your life. You deserve to travel lighter, smarter, and happier.

Make sure that the person who is hindering you is not you.

So many times, it is not "them" that stops our progress, disrupts our momentum, distracts our attention, or prevents us from accomplishing our goals—sometimes, it is US, you and me, who are the biggest deterrents to our own success.

> If you desire "Extraordinary," you can't commit to "Easy."

Stop dating or committing to things, people, or levels that minimize you. Do the work, demand the respect, and don't settle for less than what you deserve.

Everything or everyone does not deserve your time, talent, or treasure.

Do you know what deserves you? Don't invest where there is no return on investment.

It's the process that produces power.

Everything is a process, and the process is where we gain the wisdom, knowledge, and skills to be powerful. Embrace the process because the process produces the power.

Success will sometimes require that you advance without applause, labor in loneliness, struggle in silence, and press past the pain. But it is worth it.

Do what you love so that every sacrifice is worth it. Many will never understand that blessings come with burdens, miracles come with misery, and triumph comes with tribulations.

Run away from your fears, and run toward your dreams.

Are you running?

Make sure you are running in the right direction.

Success awaits!

Don't be concerned with the naysayers in the world; be concerned with the naysayers in your own head. The demons (haters, doubters, cynics, critics) IN you are more powerful than the demons around you.

What are you saying to yourself?
Your words and thoughts have power!

Resilience is a choice.
Choose to hang on to your
dreams, hold on to your
vision, and
hope on to victory.

Don't give up and don't give in
because you will win.

Nothing in life happens without action. So, move, travel, and progress toward the life you want and deserve.

You can have the life that you desire and deserve. Take action! Wishing, wondering, and whining don't create abundance; WORK does.

Victories expose vultures.

When God blesses you with any type of personal, financial, and spiritual success, expect that vultures will find you. Remember that vultures rarely attack healthy people, but they kill the emotionally wounded, the spiritually weak, and the physically wasted. Stay healthy, stay prayerful, and stay focused. Success awaits.

Don't expect something that is not on the inside to be reflected on the outside.

We have been taught to fake it until we make it. But why keep faking? Why not create who you want to be? Why not cultivate inner strength and inner beauty? Why not heal those broken parts of your soul? Why not awaken those talents and gifts that remain dormant within you?

Whatever you want to be is already inside of your head, heart, and hands.

You deserve a life of creation, not imitation.

Don't be a second-rate version of someone else;
be a first-rate original of you.

Living a lie will make you die.

When preserving your public image becomes more important than living authentically, you will eventually self-destruct.

You can't explain away bad behavior with wonderful words.

Don't offer elegant, extravagant excuses
for damnable, disgusting deeds.
It doesn't matter how you dress something up;
being low-down is still LOW DOWN.
Apologize and adjust your behavior.

Pretending will not protect, preserve, or placate you. Accept the problem and act.

Ignoring issues only intensifies them. Address issues now so that they will not cause more problems later. What you deny will only multiply.

Plan so you don't get PLAYED.

Strategy is a requirement for success: Expect and plan for the unexpected so that you will stay on course.

Some people are more concerned with the weave on your head than the love in your heart.

The superficial will never be more important than the substantial. Are you able to distinguish between the two?

There are no exits, exemptions, exceptions, or excuses in life. You must manage your own life. It is your job and your job alone.

There is no way around it. For better or worse, you are in charge! Making good decisions every day will result in a better quality of life.

There are many routes to success. Don't get caught in traffic because you are committed to only going one way.

There will be many detours on your way to your final destination. Be ready to adjust, reroute, and recalibrate. Be ready to walk, run, bike, swim, climb, hike, drive, and fly. Your path will be your own; it will not look like anyone else's journey, so let your internal GPS guide you. And even if the journey takes longer than expected, don't stop. As long as you keep moving, you will get to your destination successfully.

Stop flirting with and dating success—marry it.

Everything starts with a commitment.

Your TRUE identity is where your power lies.

Be who you are. God doesn't need
any more imposters.

Be yourself. Acting is too exhausting.

Acting like you are something that you
are not is soul-depleting.
Being yourself is soul-sustaining.
Don't drain you trying to impress them.

Climbing up is one thing.

Staying up is another.

It takes one set of skills to get you to the top, and it takes a different set of skills to keep you there. Don't get those skills confused.

Don't mistake an edge for an end.

There is a difference between an END and an EDGE! An end means completion; you are finished. An edge means that you are on to something greater, bigger, bolder, and stronger! So, don't give up! You are on the verge of a new beginning.

Just because your work is not recognized does not mean that your work is not valuable, meaningful, and important.

Your value does not need to be validated by others.

Friendships

Friends and foes look alike on the outside.

Everyone close to you is NOT clapping for you. Everyone smiling around you is NOT wishing you success. Everyone listening to your secrets is NOT loyal. Everyone helping with your dream is NOT happy about your accomplishments. Everyone by your side is NOT on your side.

Some close to you are not planning; they are plotting. They are NOT praying; they are preying. They are NOT giggling; they are gossiping. They are NOT sharing; they are stealing. They are NOT collaborating; they are competing. They are NOT connecting; they are cutting. They are NOT supporting; they are sabotaging. They are NOT meeting; they are messing.

Be careful! Sometimes the closest ones to us are hurting us the most.

Make sure that the people in your life who are supposed to be holding you up are not the ones holding you down, holding you back, or holding you hostage.

People will use all types of tactics to prevent your ascension. They will use fear, doubt, rejection, and manipulation to keep you in a place that they have determined best serves them. Watch the "holding" so that you can move forward and away quickly.

Just because they are close to you does not mean that they won't covet.

Everyone close to you is not always clapping for you. Why? Envy. Yes, jealousy happens; it's human. When you feel jealous, examine and explore the emotion because the emotion holds valuable information for your growth and development.

Our friendships should be fruitful, not fatal.

Are your friendships, relationships, and partnerships killing you? Your connections should ELEVATE you, not TERMINATE you! If your relationships are killing your spirit, threatening your dreams, and not satisfying your desires, maybe the "ships" no longer serve, support, or sustain you.

Watch who is watching you.

People who are always watching you are waiting for something. Be aware.

Looking and seeing ain't the same.

Are you really getting to know people? Do you judge on appearances alone? Why not take a moment to SEE people, because seeing others will help you truly see yourself.

It's honorable to do for others, but make sure you do for yourself first.

Are you taking care of yourself? Even though people NEED you, you NEED yourself first. Make yourself a priority in your own life. Choose you!

Some people are more concerned about your past, than your now.

Some people are more concerned about your history because they don't have the capacity to see who you are now or what you are becoming. Let them stay in the past. Your future destination is not based on their past fixation.

Don't get down like that.

Never downsize your dream, downgrade your life, or downplay your gifts just because someone is threatened by your greatness. Shine bright and encourage them to shine brightly too.

No to "down." Yes to "up."

If you want to give up something, why not give up self-doubt, self-loathing, limitations, fear, toxic people, and the quest for popularity?

All of these have a way of trapping you into places, positions, and with people who don't serve you.

Don't hang around people who always need you, but never feed you.

People should bring something to your life and not always take something from your life. Don't end up too depleted to execute your own divine assignment.

It is noble to be a "ride or die," but it is not noble to die so that you can ride.

It is admirable to be supportive. But don't let your dreams die so that you can ride with others. Nobody deserves you more than you deserve yourself. If loving someone requires that you stop loving yourself, LEAVE!

Stop following people who have demonstrated that they don't have the capacity or courage to lead.

People who lack competence, confidence, and courage don't have the ingredients to lead. Leadership is reserved for people who can make great decisions in the midst of adversity and dissention. Leadership is reserved for people who proceed without applause, acceptance, and acknowledgment. That's leadership!

If your opinion is the only opinion that matters, you will be alone—just you and your opinion.

Don't be fooled. People will not stay around if you don't respect their right to have opinions. People who can't talk will walk, and they will walk away quickly.

Sisterhood isn't based on circumstances and conditions. It's all about commitment.

Sisterhood means being there even when you don't agree with what I do, say, think, or believe. It is a decision to love, share, and care.

You can't have a healthy relationship if you are more concerned with beating her/him rather than building her/him up.

Success and growth are about cooperation and collaboration, not competition.

Relationships, professional and/or personal, cannot exist or thrive in the midst of competition.

If you want to lower the drama in your life, raise your standards of personal engagement.

Even though many people are available to you, only a few are suitable for you. The types of people you allow in your life will determine the type of engagements you have.

Qualify people!

What are your requirements?
Are your prerequisites based on your values,
virtues, and your vision for your life?
How do you select people?
Do they meet your criteria for friendships?
You must know your needs and your
non-negotiables, and you must
never compromise them.

Establish standards for entry into your life, and
make sure you select people who align with who
you are and where you want to go.
If not, you will spend the best years of your life
with the wrong people.

"Ships" that carry too much weight on one side always sink. Stay balanced in your relationships.

Mutuality and reciprocity optimize relationships. Make sure you are adding value to people who add value to you. Most importantly, make sure that what they value is what you provide.

You ain't got time for people who ain't got time for you.

Don't offer another plea. Don't make another request. You have already asked enough. Let your absence do the talking.

If people can't mentally enslave you, they will attempt to physically imprison you or emotionally control you.

Don't get tricked, tempted, or trapped by the ploys of your adversaries, haters, or self-appointed powerbrokers.
Own your own mind and guard your heart.

Be equally yoked.

Your inner circle should consist of people who are emotionally mature, spiritually equipped, and mentally sharp, so that they can walk confidently in line with your greatness.

You just can't give people what

you want to give them,

and demand they like it.

Gifts are in the eye of the beholder.
Give them what they want and what they say they
need, or don't give anything.

Some "gifts" come with a "got."

Be careful who you take gifts from. Some gifts are not treats; they are tricks. Some are not treasures; they are traps. Some are not presents; they are poison. Don't "get gotten," because you want something fast and in a hurry. Some gifts are not FREE!

Assumptions kill and steal, but questions heal. Ask!

Nothing kills relationships, families, businesses, or advancement more than assumptions! Any time we lack the patience, courage, or discipline to ask open-ended questions, we forfeit our opportunity to gain clarity, acquire wisdom, uncover the truth, walk in peace, and get what we want in life: love. Don't assume. Ask! You owe it to yourself and others.

Don't be so right that you do wrong.

"I told you so" and "you should have listened to me" will sink any "ship." Reminders of your superiority is a barrier, not a bridge, to connection.

Don't let people just drift into your life; decide who will be in your life and why.

Relationships are too critical to be casual, too major to be minor, too relevant to be reckless, too intentional to be accidental, and too powerful to be passive. They affect your life, so decide wisely.

A person in the wrong position can become your opposition.

People should be placed in positions based on their abilities. Don't make a person a confidant if they have demonstrated that they don't have the ability to exercise discretion, honor confidentiality, and exhibit emotional maturity.

Adversity always reveals who your friends are.

When you are in trouble, watch who runs away from you instead of who runs toward you. That alone will clarify who really is your friend.

People who are unwilling to stand on their own feet will always expect you to carry them.

If people don't do their part, they are not "part-ners"; they are parasites.

Being physically close is not the same as being emotionally connected.

Just because a person is by your side does not mean that they are on your side.

Don't be concerned about who is talking about you; be more concerned about who is listening, repeating, and adding more flavor to what is being said.

Your friends should be shutting down gossip,

not spreading it.

Don't get in the "ship" if you don't have the desire nor the capacity to relate.

If you are not interested in doing what it takes to be connected personally or professionally, fly solo. "Ships" require energy and maintenance.

Being electronically connected is not the same as being emotionally close.

Be connected to everyone but only be close to a few.

Just because people "liked" your Facebook post does not mean that they "like" you.

Don't let your self-esteem, self-acceptance, and your self-love be determined by computer clicks.

You don't eat, sleep, live with or befriend snakes, rats, or roaches; you kill them!

Dr. Maya Angelou told us: "when people show you who they are, believe them".

Relationships

> If you can't be seen, be heard, or be known in a relationship, do yourself a favor and be gone.

If you are paying attention to someone who is no longer paying attention to you, leave. You are too valuable to be ignored.

If you reserve common courtesies such as "Thank you," "You're welcome," "Please," "May I," and other civilities for people other than your partner, you may not be ready for a relationship.

Your partner deserves your best manners and your best communication skills. Don't give strangers your best. Your best goes to God, you, and then your beloved.

If you are in a relationship that makes you feel physically sick, spiritually bankrupt, emotionally drained, socially isolated, and financially depleted, you may need to leave your relationship.

Some endings are necessary. Some endings need to happen today so that you can create a better, more desirous future for TOMORROW! There is no shame in saying "No" to chronic hurt, constant abuse, and endless disappointment.

If you are concerned about what others say about your relationship, you're not ready for a relationship.

It is not your concern or your business what people say about your relationship. Nor is it your responsibility to manage people's perceptions either. Don't share your intimate details with people who don't have relationship expertise, or people who are not invested in your staying together And don't invite people into your private spaces. It is not their "ship," so don't invite them aboard.

If you are not willing to admit and address your contribution to a problem, maybe you're not ready for a relationship.

You are always part of the problem and part of the solution. If you must point fingers, point at yourself first.

If you choose to be in a relationship with someone who has demonstrated that they don't have the capacity or the desire to live in integrity, you are not a victim of abuse, you are a volunteer.

You can volunteer for many things, but never volunteer for your own abuse or degradation. If a person consistently demonstrates that they don't have the desire nor the expertise to honor you, honor yourself and LEAVE!

If you are willing to make relationship decisions from a place of inspiration and not from a place of desperation, you may be ready for a relationship.

"Needing" is one thing, but being "needy" is another. Remember, it is difficult to be in a relationship with someone who is emotionally needy and emotionally greedy. You don't need a person who only needs you; you also need someone who feeds you with advice, encouragement, and inspiration.

Are you being fed?

Do you have what it takes? If not, do the work. You can't perform what you don't practice.

Three things are required to give your relationship the best chance for survival: Wisdom (knowledge about when, where, how, and why you make decisions), Ways (skills, tools, and techniques that help with communication, collaboration, and connection), and the Will (discipline, self-control, and commitment).

If you bring your old assumptions and your old perspectives into a new relationship, you may not be ready for a new partner.

If you have a new love, get some new data. Don't repeat patterns that already resulted in failure. Get and apply new information to support your relationship success.

If you expect your partner to accommodate or compensate for your pathology, your dysfunction, or your lack of ambition, you may not be ready for a relationship.

Nobody should make room for you to self-destruct, nobody should accommodate your addictions, and nobody should compensate for your laziness. Your partner is not a crutch. Your partner needs a person, not a project.

If your ego is so fragile that you cannot withstand challenge, review, scrutiny, disappointment, or delay, you may not be ready for a relationship.

Is your EGO running amok? EGO, as in Ending Growth Opportunities. If your EGO is too big, there may be little room to accommodate a relationship.

If you're not willing to engage in healthy conflicts to address differences and grievances in a constructive way, you may not be ready for a relationship.

Our greatest connections can result from our greatest conflicts, if those conflicts are handled in a loving, constructive way. Are you ready to handle conflict so that you can live and love in greater abundance? Or do you just want to fight and fail?

If you are expected to be bland versus brilliant, mediocre versus magnificent, stagnant versus successful, complacent versus competent, ignorant versus intelligent, and/or idle versus industrious, you may not be ready for a relationship.

Are you TOO Big, TOO Bold, or TOO Brilliant for some relationships? If you are downplaying your strengths, downsizing your dreams, downgrading your desires, or stalling your success, your relationship is TOO small for you. If you are shrinking to accommodate or compensate for your mate's insecurity, inactivity, or incompetence, you are only hurting yourself!

If you prefer to talk about your mate than to talk to your mate, you may not be ready for a relationship.

Are you talking to the person who can correct the problem or talking to the person who can create more problems? Only you can decide.

If you prefer to assume something rather than ask about something, you may not be ready for a relationship.

If you want to destroy your relationships, keep thinking that you know all there is to know about your partner. Always ask! Then, ask again. You don't know everything because your partner is constantly evolving.

If you don't know what you emotionally, spiritually, physically, sexually, or intellectually want in a relationship, and you are not open to exploration, you may not be ready for a relationship.

YOUR job is to know yourself well enough so that you can educate someone else about your needs, dreams, and desires. You write your OWN user's guide—don't expect someone to know it or write it for you.

If you would prefer to get mad at your partner rather than be informed by your partner, you may not be ready for a relationship.

If you are not interested in learning about someone, stay single.

The goal isn't to be right. The goal is to get it right in a way that honors both of you.

So often we will stoop to any level to win a fight. But is winning the ultimate goal? If winning an argument causes you to lose your partner's love, respect, and devotion, what have you really won? Something to consider, right?

Until you realize that your presence, attention, and love are valuable contributions, you will sell yourself short.

You MUST VALUE yourself, so that you can teach and train others to value you, too. Know your worth.

The most important things in life must be built, not bought. Build wisely.

You can buy a one-night stand, but you have to build a long-term relationship. You can buy muscles, but you have to build inner strength. You can buy make-up, but you have to build inner beauty. You can buy a church, but you have to build faith. Yes, the most important things in life must be built not bought. So, build wisely.

If money is the only currency you value, then you'll always be broke.

Money can buy you things, but not the things that really matter, like love, empathy, support, encouragement, commitment, peace, truth, a tight embrace, a timely call, and a shoulder to cry on. Real wealth includes deep relationships.

Stop wanting what doesn't want you.

You don't have to beg for anything.

You choose you.

If you don't want to grow up, don't show up.

Relationships are for grown folks willing to do the emotional work.

Don't expect from a relationship what you fail to put into it.

You must bring it to get it.

Don't let the distance get further than your arms can reach.

Handle issues when they are small. Delay brings decay and makes people stray.

Love is never enough to sustain a relationship.

Don't enter a relationship empty-handed, empty-hearted, and empty-headed. People want connection AND contribution.

About the Author

SharRon Jamison, MBA
Inspirational Speaker, Minister,
Life Strategist, Entrepreneur, Author

SharRon Jamison is the founder/CEO of The Jamison Group, a leadership, relationship, and empowerment training company. Her desire is for people to "Dare To Soar Higher" in their personal and professional lives.

SharRon received a BA from Hampton University in Hampton, Virginia, then moved forward to earn her MBA from Nova Southeastern University, and is currently pursuing her MDiv degree at the Interdenominational Theological Center in Atlanta, Georgia.

SharRon is an international speaker, empathetic life coach, business professional, licensed minister, proud mother, and author of three books: *I Can Depend on Me, I Have Learned A Few Things* and *The Strength of My Soul: Stories of Sisterhood, and Triumph and Inspiration.*

She is also the contributing author in three upcoming anthologies: *I Bared My Chest, The Unstoppable Woman of Purpose*, and Kim Coles's *Open The G.I.F.T.S.*

Her newest book, *50 Choices to a Fulfilling Life*, is scheduled for release in early 2017.

Connect with SharRon Jamison at
www.SharRonJamison.com

or on social media under her name.

CREATING DISTINCTIVE BOOKS
WITH INTENTIONAL RESULTS

We're a collaborative group of creative masterminds with a mission to produce high-quality books to position you for monumental success in the marketplace.

Our professional team of writers, editors, designers, and marketing strategists work closely together to ensure that every detail of your book is a clear representation of the message in your writing.

Want to know more?
Write to us at info@publishyourgift.com
or call (888) 949-6228

Discover great books, exclusive offers, and more at
www.PublishYourGift.com

Connect with us on social media

@publishyourgift

www.ingramcontent.com/pod-product-compliance
Lightning Source LLC
Chambersburg PA
CBHW071620080526
44588CB00010B/1201